IN the busy rain forest of Malaysia, a grasshopper leaps into a spray of orchids. Suddenly, one of the "flowers" turns on the grasshopper. An orchid mantis, with wings like petals, grips it tightly. For the grasshopper, there will be no escape.

▲ The colors of the Solomon Island leaf frog match those of the forest floor. The shape of its head, with its horn-like protrusions, resembles that of a leaf.

The orchid mantis is a master of camouflage—the art of hiding while in plain sight. Camouflage enables predators like the orchid mantis to hide while they lie in wait for their prey. For other animals, camouflage is a method of protection from their enemies.

Animals blend into the background in several ways. Their colors and patterns may match their surroundings. The shape of their bodies may resemble some other object, such as a stick, a leaf, or a flower. Crests and frills may break up the outline of their bodies, disguising their real shape and fooling the eye. They may even behave like something else—a fluttering leaf or a dangerous animal, for example.

▶ The color and pattern of this owl's feathers blend in with a background of tree bark.

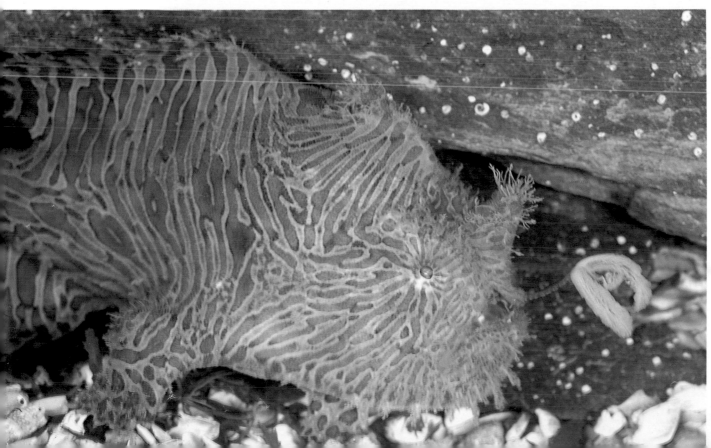

◀ Frills and crests, together with a confusing pattern of stripes, help hide the "fish shape" of this anglerfish, making it hard to spot in its home in the Coral Sea near Australia.

Some animals depend on color alone for concealment. The skin of the red-eyed tree frog is the universal green of the rain forest. Others use both color and pattern. The comet moth matches the colors and patterns of the drying leaves of the undergrowth.

◄ Red-eyed tree frog (Panama).

▼ Comet moths (Madagascar).

6

The Kenyan sand boa snuggles into the ground and depends on its coloration and pattern to hide as it pokes its head out from among a pile of stones.

Sand dabs use the same technique underwater. These fish settle on the sand and flutter their fins to partially bury themselves. Soon only a faint fish "shadow" remains.

▲ Sand boa.

▼ Sand dab.

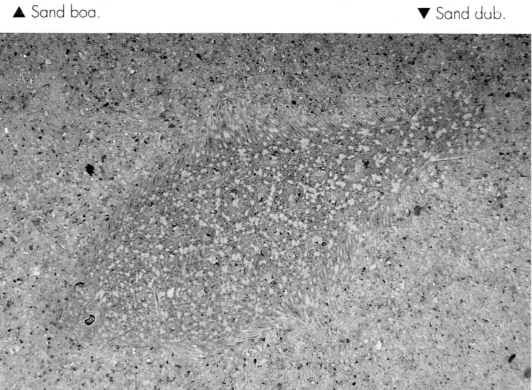

◀ With its startling colors and pattern, this dragon eel could be mistaken for part of the coral reef.

Brightly colored animals can be masters of camouflage. Scorpionfish, warbonnets, and other tropical fish look shocking in open water, but when swimming in the reef, they match the vivid tints of the coral. As well as being camouflaged by their colors, these fish are also hidden by their complicated shapes: with their jagged outlines and frilled fins, they look "unfishlike" among the coral branches. When a predator looks for a fish shape, its eyes detect only bits and pieces.

▶ Japanese decorated warbonnets.

▼ Scorpionfish.

▲ Hawkfish (Coral Sea, Australia).

▶ Zebras (Kenya).

The striped hawkfish has bright bands of color that break up its outline and fool predators in a similar way. This technique is called "disruptive coloration."

Zebras also benefit from disruptive coloration. Although they are easy to see on the grasslands at noon, at dawn and dusk their stripes make them harder to see. Since lions and other predators prefer to hunt in low light, the pattern helps the zebra survive.

▲ Jewel chameleon (Madagascar).

Chameleons are famous for their ability to change color. However, they don't change color in order to match their surroundings. Their usual color matches the place they live; they *change* color to communicate with other chameleons. When they change color, they become more noticeable, not less.

Chameleons combine many camouflage techniques. Their flat, oval shape resembles a leaf, and many species grow crests along the edges of the oval to hide their chameleon shape. They spend most of the day motionless except for swiveling their eyes to look for food. But when they do walk or climb, they rock back and forth so their movements seem as random as those of a leaf in the breeze.

▼ Casque-headed chameleon (Kenya).

The leaf-tail gecko shares the rain forest of Madagascar with several species of chameleon. A flat reptile with jagged frills and a broad tail, it clings with its disk-like toes to tree trunks that are mottled with lichen (tiny plants that grow on rocks and trees). Gradually, the gecko's skin changes to the color and pattern of the lichen patches. Within twenty minutes, the lizard seems part of the tree. Its frills help to break up its outline. Then, when an insect flies near, the gecko leaps into the air and snatches it with its jaws.

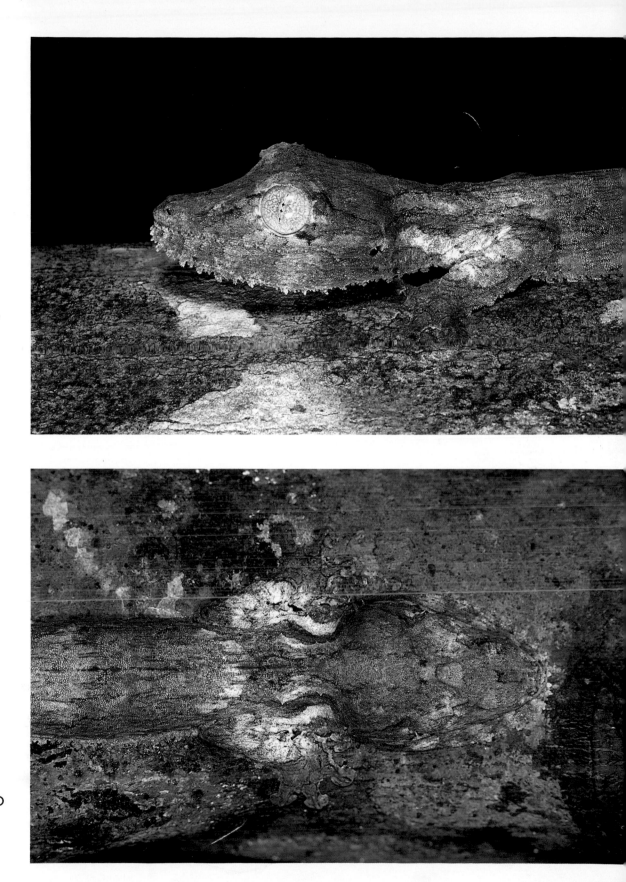

Caught against a background of brown trees in Montana, a snowshoe hare in its winter coat stands out plainly. Against the white of a snowfield, it almost disappears.

Animals in cooler climates change with the seasons. Summer camouflage is often useless when winter snow changes the green and brown forests and fields to white, so many birds and animals turn white in the winter.

The snowshoe hare wears a drab brown in summer but changes to white for the winter. If it did not change, it would be an easy target for foxes and birds of prey. Ptarmigans—slow, squat birds that live in the same parts of the northern United States and Canada as the snowshoe hare—use identical tactics, switching from brown to white and back again as the seasons change.

▶ *Above:* White-tailed ptarmigan in winter (Washington State). *Below:* Willow ptarmigan in summer (Alaska).

The most dangerous time of any animal's life is babyhood, and baby animals have some of the most effective camouflage. The mottled pattern of a fawn (a young deer) makes it hard for predators to see. Baby chameleons wear the color of tree bark—dull browns and grays—turning leaf green only when they are large enough to mimic a leaf.

◀ Blacktail fawn (Washington State).

▶ Western sandpiper's eggs (Alaska).

Birds' eggs are often colored to match their surroundings, camouflaging the baby birds even before they are born. Once born, baby birds are usually a gray puff of feathers, difficult to see in the nest. When they reach adulthood, they will acquire the more colorful plumage of their parents.

▶ Baby night herons
(Falkland Islands).

◀ Baby pardalis chameleon.

▲ Walking stick (Malaysia).

Some animals don't simply blend into the background: they pretend to be something they're not—part of a plant, or another animal. In the tropical rain forest, many insects survive disguised as parts of plants. Among them are many species of walking stick. Some look like bare sticks; others resemble dead twigs with dried leaves attached.

The jungles of the world are full of leaf insects. The most common are bright green and have broad, flat bodies. They wander slowly among the leafy underbrush searching for food.

▼ Leaf insect (Malaysia).

Animals in disguise must act the part. When walking sticks aren't walking, they are difficult to see. If they run, predators will suspect a trick. A chameleon wouldn't be mistaken for a leaf if it hopped like a kangaroo, so chameleons move slowly, rocking like a leaf in the breeze.

◀ Some insects imitate dead leaves. It's easy to miss this arsenura moth of Panama as it rests on a carpet of fallen leaves.

▶ In addition to the orchid mantis (*page 3*), many species of mantis put on convincing disguises. *Above:* The dead-leaf mantis of Malaysia hides on the forest floor. *Below:* The yellow-leaf mantis of Panama hides among fallen leaves, waiting for another insect to come close enough to eat.

For animals that mimic other animals, every day is Halloween—they pretend to be fearsome beasts! By adopting the color and shape of dangerous animals, they fool predators into leaving them alone.

In the jungles of Central America, a brown caterpillar lives among the brown leaves of the forest floor. When noticed by an enemy, the caterpillar turns, revealing two black spots that look like snake eyes. Startled predators usually decide to leave the caterpillar alone.

A caterpillar in the Panamanian rain forest, with its two snake-eye-like spots.

▲ King snake.

At first glance, the bright, glossy red-and-black bands of the king snake resemble those of a coral snake. Because coral snakes have a very poisonous bite, most animals steer clear of them. By mimicking the coral snake, the harmless king snake benefits from their caution.

Unlike animals that depend on camouflage for defense, larger camouflaged hunters have little to fear from other animals. They employ camouflage only to avoid detection when they hunt.

Even though they are the largest carnivore on earth, growing to over a thousand pounds in weight, white polar bears on the snow will escape notice by all but the keenest eye. On an overcast day, or during a storm, the first sign of an approaching bear is the swinging of its black nose against the white background.

◀ Leopard (South Africa).

Anyone could spot a leopard walking down the street—but in the dry grasses of Africa the leopard almost disappears. The harsh African sun casts dark shadows in the grass, which are matched by the leopard's black spots and tan fur. By the time an antelope or other prey notices the leopard, it's often too late.

◀ Gaboon vipers (central Africa).

The velvety skin of the Gaboon viper resembles dead leaves. It lives on the soggy jungle floor of the Congo Basin in central Africa. Sunlight is blocked by a snarl of branches and leaves far above and seldom brightens the forest floor. Encountering this snake is a nasty surprise for any animal—including man. It has the longest fangs of any snake, over two inches long, and its venom kills swiftly.

▶ The colors of many species of big cat effectively camouflage them in their hunting grounds. *Above:* A puma hides among the dry colors of Arizona. *Below:* A lynx blends in with a tree trunk in British Columbia, Canada.

When we notice an animal concealing itself through color, pattern, or mimicry, we are looking at part of the competition between hunters and the hunted. Of course, camouflage is difficult to see. But if our eyes are sharp enough, what we can see is a powerful weapon in the struggle for survival.

Camouflaged predators and camouflaged prey: Among the universal green of the South American rain forest, a green tree snake suddenly devours a green frog. In southern Africa, a leopard rests with a freshly killed bush hare.

Index

Page numbers in **bold** type refer to illustrations.

anglerfish, **5**
arsenura moth, **22**

baby animals, 18-19
blacktail deer, **18**
bush hare, **31**

casque-headed chameleon, **13**
caterpillar, 24, **24**
colors, as camouflage, 4-19, 21, 24-27, 30-31, 32
comet moth, 6, **6**
coral snake, 25
crests, as camouflage, 4, **5**, 13

dead-leaf mantis, **23**
disruptive coloration, 10
dragon eel, **8**

frills, as camouflage, 4, **5**, 8, 15

Gaboon viper, 28, **29**

hawkfish, 10, **10**
heron, **19**

Japanese decorated warbonnet, **9**
jewel chameleon, **12**

Kenyan sand boa, 7, **7**
king snake, 25, **25**

leaf insects, 21, **21**
leaf-tail gecko, 14-15
leopard, 28, **28**, **31**
lynx, **29**

motion and motionlessness, as camouflage, 13

night heron, **19**

orchid mantis, **2-3**, 3-4
owl, **5**

pardalis chameleon, **18**
patterns, as camouflage, 4, **5**, 7, **8**, 18, 31, 32
polar bear, **26-27**, 27
predators, 4, 8, 10, 27, 31
pretending (mimicry), as camouflage, 20-25, 31
prey, 4, 28, 31
ptarmigans, 17, **17**
puma, **29**

red-eyed tree frog, 6, **6**

sand dab, 7, **7**
scorpionfish, 8, **9**
seasons, and camouflage, 17
shape, body, as camouflage, 4, **4**, 8, 13, 24
snowshoe hare, **16**, 17
Solomon Island leaf frog, **4**

walking stick, 20, **20**, 23
warbonnets, 8, **9**
Western sandpiper, **19**

yellow-leaf mantis, **23**

zebras, 10, **10-11**

NATURAL SELECTION   Animal camouflage is one of the many results of a process called "natural selection." As one generation of a species follows another, chance variations among individuals occur—just as some people in the same family have darker eyes or larger noses than others. In the animal kingdom, some of these variations—for example, a color or pattern that enables an individual to hide better—can increase its chances for survival. Animals with lucky variations tend to survive and to pass these variations on to their children. Animals without the variations tend to die out.

Scientists have studied camouflage and natural selection at work among insects. In England, a group of pale-colored moths hid on the pale bark of trees. With the arrival of industry in the area where the moths lived, soot from factory chimneys stained the trees. Birds were able to find the light-colored moths easily against the stained trees and eat them. But by chance some moths were born dark-colored. They and their dark-colored offspring were better able to survive than the pale moths. Eventually, most of the moths in the area were dark-colored.

Scientists could see this happening because the life span of the moth is short and many generations can be born in just a few years. As a result, adaptations can appear relatively quickly. In longer-lived animals, similar adaptations might take centuries or more to appear.

ABOUT THE AUTHOR AND PHOTOGRAPHER   James Martin and Art Wolfe are the author and photographer of *Chameleons: Dragons in the Trees,* named a Notable Book for Children by the American Library Association, an Outstanding Science Trade Book for Children by the National Science Teachers' Association, and an Outstanding Nature Book by the John Burroughs Association. James Martin is also the author of *Tentacles: The Amazing World of Octopus, Squid, and Their Relatives,* as well as a book for adults about chameleons and articles for *Smithsonian, Sports Illustrated,* and other publications. He lives in Seattle. Art Wolfe is one of America's most distinguished and widely published nature photographers. He has photographed many books, including studies of owls and bears and a survey of North American wildlife entitled *The Kingdom.* His work has appeared in numerous magazines and journals. He also lives in Seattle.